Cash on Delivery (Contre Remboursement)

The Postal History of France – Vol. 1

Copyright © 2015 by Martin Nicholson

Martin Nicholson
Church Stretton
Shropshire SY6 7DQ
United Kingdom

Email – newbinaries@yahoo.co.uk

From the viewpoint of the postal historian the Cash on Delivery (Contre Remboursement) service that operated between 1920 and 1957 was of particular interest.

1. The COD letter-card (carte-lettre remboursement or CLR) can be found bearing the standard postage rate of the day or the standard rate plus the additional postage required for registration. Both of these options also exist with and without evidence of the presentation tax that needed to be paid on an undelivered item.
2. The COD postcard (carte postale remboursement or CPR) was introduced in 1935 and can be found bearing the standard postage rate of the day or the standard rate plus the additional postage required for registration. Both of these options also exist with and without evidence of the presentation tax that needed to be paid on an undelivered item.
3. The Cash on Delivery service was also available without the need to use the dedicated postal stationery.
4. Taking 1947 as an example. There are 8 different combinations of CLR/CPR, non-registered/registered and with and without the presentation tax for each of the 4 different "rate band eras" (some very short lived) that existed.

0.25	1st October 1920 to 15th July 1925	COD letter-card (CLR)
0.30	16 July 1925 to 30th April 1926	COD letter-card (CLR)
0.40	1st May 1926 to 8th August 1926	COD letter-card (CLR)
0.40	1st September 1935 to 11th July 1937	COD postcard (CPR)
0.50	9th August 1926 to 11th July 1937	COD letter-card (CLR)
0.55	12th July 1937 to 16th November 1938	COD postcard (CPR)
0.55	1st October 1920 to 15th July 1925	Undelivered COD letter-card (CLR)
0.60	1st October 1920 to 24th March 1924	Registered COD letter-card (CLR)
0.65	12th July 1937 to 16th November 1938	COD letter-card (CLR)
0.70	17th November 1938 to 30th November 1939	COD postcard (CPR)
0.70	16 July 1925 to 30th April 1926	Undelivered COD letter-card (CLR)
0.80	1st December 1939 to 4th January 1942	COD postcard (CPR)
0.85	25th March 1924 to 15th July 1925	Registered COD letter-card (CLR)
0.90	1st October 1920 to 24th March 1924	Undelivered registered COD letter-card (CLR)
0.90	17th November 1938 to 30th November 1939	COD letter-card (CLR)
0.90	1st May 1926 to 8th August 1926	Undelivered COD letter-card (CLR)
1.00	1st December 1939 to 4th January 1942	COD letter-card (CLR)
1.05	16 July 1925 to 30th April 1926	Registered COD letter-card (CLR)
1.10	9th August 1926 to 8th April 1931	Undelivered COD letter-card (CLR)
1.15	25th March 1924 to 15th July 1925	Undelivered registered COD letter-card (CLR)
1.20	5th January 1942 to 28th February 1945	COD postcard (CPR)
1.40	1st May 1926 to 8th August 1926	Registered COD letter-card (CLR)
1.40	1st September 1935 to 11th July 1937	Undelivered COD postcard (CPR)
1.45	16 July 1925 to 30th April 1926	Undelivered registered COD letter-card (CLR)
1.50	5th January 1942 to 28th February 1945	COD letter-card (CLR)
1.50	1st March 1945 to 31st December 1945	COD postcard (CPR)
1.50	9th August 1926 to 17th July 1932	Registered COD letter-card (CLR)
1.50	9th April 1931 to 11th July 1957	Undelivered COD letter-card (CLR)
1.55	12th July 1937 to 16th November 1938	Undelivered COD postcard (CPR)
1.65	1st September 1935 to 11th July 1937	Registered COD postcard (CPR)
1.65	12th July 1937 to 16th November 1938	Undelivered COD letter-card (CLR)
1.70	17th November 1938 to 30th November 1939	Undelivered COD postcard (CPR)
1.75	18th July 1932 to 11th July 1937	Registered COD letter-card (CLR)
1.80	1st December 1939 to 4th January 1942	Undelivered COD postcard (CPR)
1.90	17th November 1938 to 30th November 1939	Undelivered COD letter-card (CLR)
1.90	1st May 1926 to 8th August 1926	Undelivered registered COD letter-card (CLR)
2.00	1st March 1945 to 31st December 1945	COD letter-card (CLR)
2.00	1st December 1939 to 4th January 1942	Undelivered COD letter-card (CLR)
2.05	12th July 1937 to 16th November 1938	Registered COD postcard (CPR)
2.10	9th August 1926 to 8th April 1931	Undelivered registered COD letter-card (CLR)
2.15	12th July 1937 to 16th November 1938	Registered COD letter-card (CLR)
2.30	17th November 1938 to 30th November 1939	Registered COD postcard (CPR)
2.50	1st January 1946 to 31st December 1946	COD postcard (CPR)
2.50	17th November 1938 to 30th November 1939	Registered COD letter-card (CLR)
2.50	9th April 1931 to 17th July 1932	Undelivered registered COD letter-card (CLR)
2.65	1st September 1935 to 11th July 1937	Undelivered registered COD postcard (CPR)
2.70	5th January 1942 to 28th February 1945	Undelivered COD postcard (CPR)
2.75	18th July 1932 to 11th July 1937	Undelivered registered COD letter-card (CLR)
2.80	1st December 1939 to 4th January 1942	Registered COD postcard (CPR)
3.00	1st January 1946 to 31st December 1946	COD letter-card (CLR)
3.00	1st December 1939 to 4th January 1942	Registered COD letter-card (CLR)
3.00	5th January 1942 to 28th February 1945	Undelivered COD letter-card (CLR)
3.05	12th July 1937 to 16th November 1938	Undelivered registered COD postcard (CPR)
3.15	12th July 1937 to 16th November 1938	Undelivered registered COD letter-card (CLR)

3.30	17th November 1938 to 30th November 1939	Undelivered registered COD postcard (CPR)
3.50	1st March 1947 to 7th July 1947	COD postcard (CPR)
3.50	17th November 1938 to 30th November 1939	Undelivered registered COD letter-card (CLR)
3.80	2nd January 1947 to 28th February 1947	COD postcard (CPR)
3.80	1st December 1939 to 4th January 1942	Undelivered registered COD postcard (CPR)
4.00	1st January 1947 only	COD postcard (CPR)
4.00	1st December 1939 to 4th January 1942	Undelivered registered COD letter-card (CLR)
4.20	5th January 1942 to 28th February 1945	Registered COD postcard (CPR)
4.50	2nd January 1947 to 7th July 1947	COD letter-card (CLR)
4.50	5th January 1942 to 28th February 1945	Registered COD letter-card (CLR)
4.50	1st March 1945 to 31st December 1945	Undelivered COD postcard (CPR)
5.00	1st January 1947 only	COD letter-card (CLR)
5.00	8th July 1947 to 20th September 1948	COD postcard (CPR)
5.00	1st March 1945 to 31st December 1945	Undelivered COD letter-card (CLR)
5.50	1st March 1945 to 31st December 1945	Registered COD postcard (CPR)
5.70	5th January 1942 to 28th February 1945	Undelivered registered COD postcard (CPR)
6.00	8th July 1947 to 20th September 1948	COD letter-card (CLR)
6.00	1st March 1945 to 31st December 1945	Registered COD letter-card (CLR)
6.00	5th January 1942 to 28th February 1945	Undelivered registered COD letter-card (CLR)
7.50	1st January 1946 to 31st December 1946	Undelivered COD postcard (CPR)
8.00	21st September 1948 to 5th January 1949	COD postcard (CPR)
8.00	1st January 1946 to 31st December 1946	Undelivered COD letter-card (CLR)
8.50	1st January 1946 to 31st December 1946	Registered COD postcard (CPR)
8.50	1st March 1945 to 31st December 1945	Undelivered registered COD postcard (CPR)
9.00	1st January 1946 to 31st December 1946	Registered COD letter-card (CLR)
9.00	1st March 1945 to 31st December 1945	Undelivered registered COD letter-card (CLR)
10.00	21st September 1948 to 5th January 1949	COD letter-card (CLR)
10.50	1st March 1947 to 7th July 1947	Undelivered COD postcard (CPR)
11.30	2nd January 1947 to 28th February 1947	Undelivered COD postcard (CPR)
11.50	1st March 1947 to 7th July 1947	Undelivered COD letter-card (CLR)
12.00	6th January 1949 to 30th June 1957	COD postcard (CPR)
12.00	2nd January 1947 to 28th February 1947	Undelivered COD letter-card (CLR)
12.00	1st January 1947 only	Undelivered COD postcard (CPR)
12.50	1st March 1947 to 7th July 1947	Registered COD postcard (CPR)
13.00	1st January 1947 only	Undelivered COD letter-card (CLR)
13.30	2nd January 1947 to 28th February 1947	Registered COD postcard (CPR)
13.50	1st March 1947 to 7th July 1947	Registered COD letter-card (CLR)
13.50	1st January 1946 to 31st December 1946	Undelivered registered COD postcard (CPR)
14.00	2nd January 1947 to 28th February 1947	Registered COD letter-card (CLR)
14.00	1st January 1947 only	Registered COD postcard (CPR)
14.00	1st January 1946 to 31st December 1946	Undelivered registered COD letter-card (CLR)
15.00	6th January 1949 to 30th June 1957	COD letter-card (CLR)
15.00	1st January 1947 only	Registered COD letter-card (CLR)
15.00	8th July 1947 to 20th September 1948	Undelivered COD postcard (CPR)
16.00	8th July 1947 to 20th September 1948	Undelivered COD letter-card (CLR)
19.00	8th July 1947 to 20th September 1948	Registered COD postcard (CPR)
19.50	1st March 1947 to 7th July 1947	Undelivered registered COD postcard (CPR)
20.00	8th July 1947 to 20th September 1948	Registered COD letter-card (CLR)
20.50	1st March 1947 to 7th July 1947	Undelivered registered COD letter-card (CLR)
20.80	2nd January 1947 to 28th February 1947	Undelivered registered COD postcard (CPR)
21.50	2nd January 1947 to 28th February 1947	Undelivered registered COD letter-card (CLR)
22.00	1st January 1947 only	Undelivered registered COD postcard (CPR)
23.00	21st September 1948 to 5th January 1949	Undelivered COD postcard (CPR)
23.00	1st January 1947 only	Undelivered registered COD letter-card (CLR)

25.00	21st September 1948 to 5th January 1949	Undelivered COD letter-card (CLR)
29.00	8th July 1947 to 20th September 1948	Undelivered registered COD postcard (CPR)
30.00	8th July 1947 to 20th September 1948	Undelivered registered COD letter-card (CLR)
32.00	6th January 1949 to 7th September 1951	Undelivered COD postcard (CPR)
33.00	21st September 1948 to 5th January 1949	Registered COD postcard (CPR)
35.00	21st September 1948 to 5th January 1949	Registered COD letter-card (CLR)
35.00	6th January 1949 to 7th December 1951	Undelivered COD letter-card (CLR)
37.00	8th December 1951 to 30th June 1957	Undelivered COD postcard (CPR)
40.00	8th December 1951 to 30th June 1957	Undelivered COD letter-card (CLR)
47.00	1st July 1949 to 30th June 1957	Registered COD postcard (CPR)
48.00	21st September 1948 to 5th January 1949	Undelivered registered COD postcard (CPR)
50.00	1st July 1949 to 30th June 1957	Registered COD letter-card (CLR)
50.00	21st September 1948 to 5th January 1949	Undelivered registered COD letter-card (CLR)
62.00	6th January 1949 to 30th June 1949	Registered COD postcard (CPR)
65.00	6th January 1949 to 30th June 1949	Registered COD letter-card (CLR)
67.00	1st July 1949 to 7th December 1951	Undelivered registered COD postcard (CPR)
70.00	1st July 1949 to 7th December 1951	Undelivered registered COD letter-card (CLR)
72.00	8th December 1951 to 30th June 1957	Undelivered registered COD postcard (CPR)
75.00	8th December 1951 to 30th June 1957	Undelivered registered COD letter-card (CLR)
82.00	6th January 1949 to 30th June 1949	Undelivered registered COD postcard (CPR)
85.00	6th January 1949 to 30th June 1949	Undelivered registered COD letter-card (CLR)

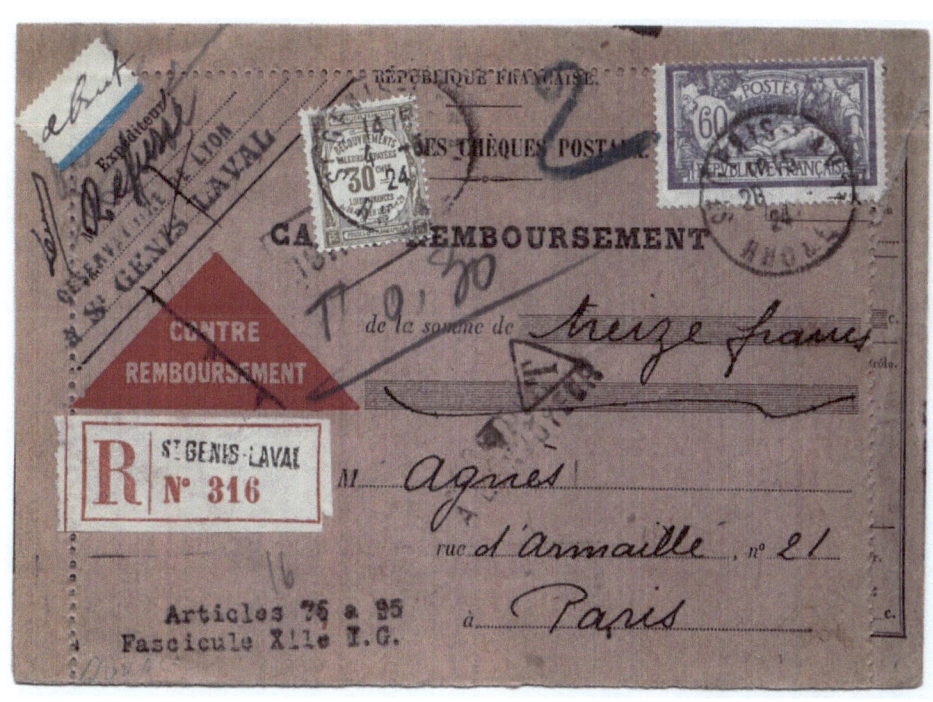

0.90F rate - 1st October 1920 to 24th March 1924

Undelivered registered COD letter-card (carte-lettre remboursement or CLR)

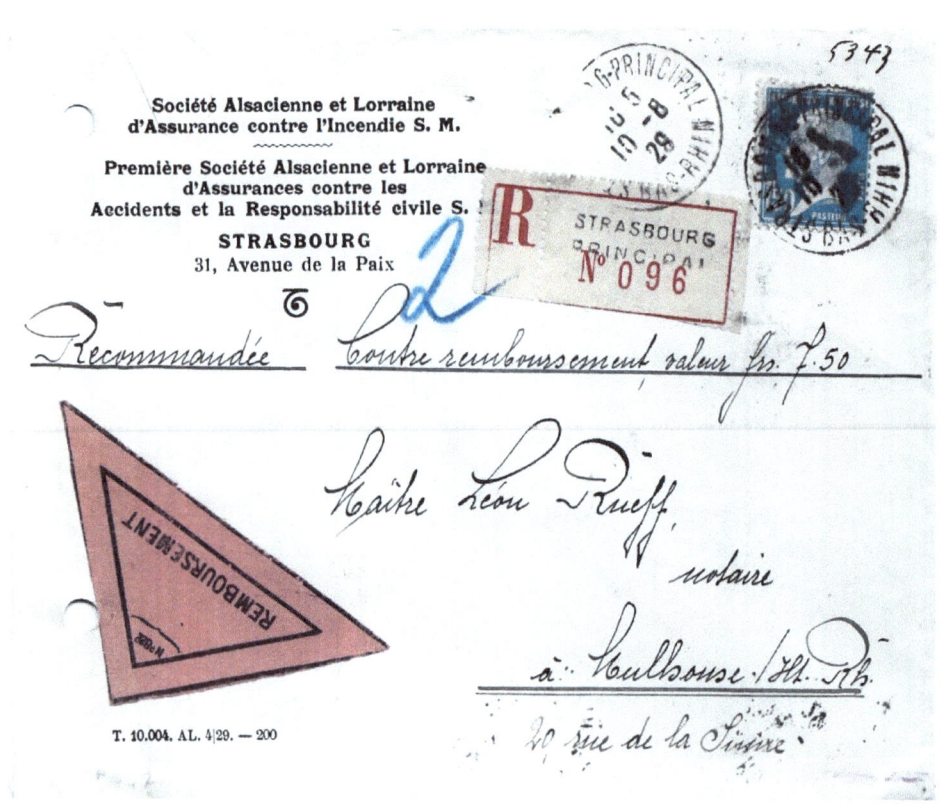

1.50F rate - 9th August 1926 to 17th July 1932

Registered COD letter

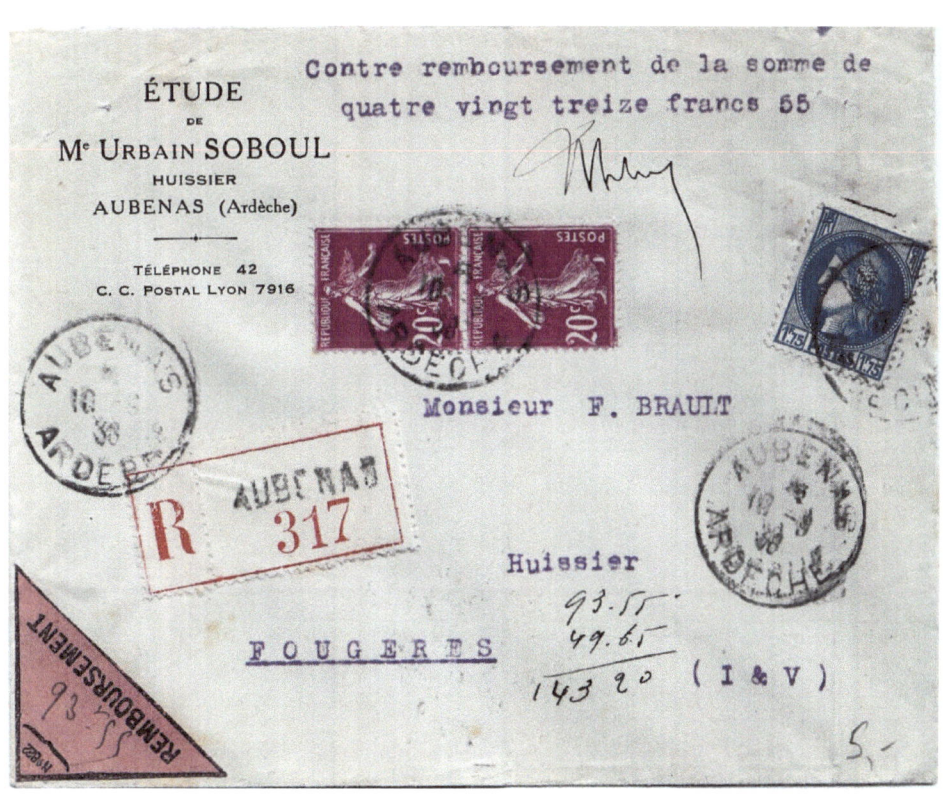

2.15F rate - 12th July 1937 to 16th November 1938

Registered COD letter

2.15F rate - 12th July 1937 to 16th November 1938

Registered COD letter-card (carte-lettre remboursement or CLR)

2.75F rate - 18th July 1932 to 11th July 1937

Undelivered registered COD letter

3.50F rate - 17th November 1938 to 30th November 1939

Undelivered registered COD letter-card (carte-lettre remboursement or CLR)

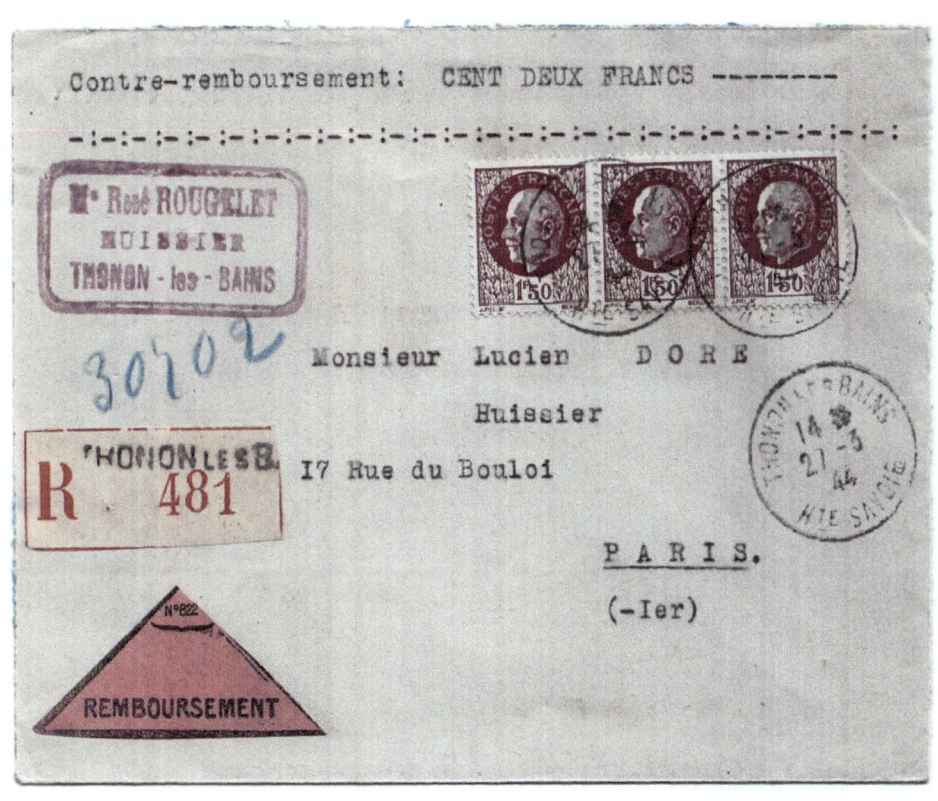

4.50 F rate - 5th January 1942 to 28th February 1945

Registered COD letter

12F rate - 6th January 1949 to 30th June 1957

COD postcard (carte postale remboursement or CPR)

12F rate - 6th January 1949 to 30th June 1957

COD postcard (carte postale remboursement or CPR)

12F rate - 6th January 1949 to 30th June 1957

COD postcard (carte postale remboursement or CPR)

32F rate - 6th January 1949 to 7th September 1951

Undelivered COD postcard (carte postale remboursement or CPR)

32F rate - 6th January 1949 to 7th September 1951

Undelivered COD postcard (carte postale remboursement or CPR)

32F rate - 6th January 1949 to 7th September 1951

Undelivered COD postcard (carte postale remboursement or CPR)

37F rate - 8th December 1951 to 30th June 1957

Undelivered COD postcard (carte postale remboursement or CPR)

40F rate - 8th December 1951 to 30th June 1957

Undelivered COD letter-card (carte-lettre remboursement or CLR)

35F +5F rate - 21st September 1948 to 5th January 1949

Registered COD letter, 2nd weight band

65F rate - 6th January 1949 to 30th June 1949

Registered COD letter

65F rate - 6th January 1949 to 30th June 1949

Registered COD letter-card (carte-lettre remboursement or CLR)

75F rate - 8th December 1951 to 30th June 1957

Undelivered registered COD letter-card (carte-lettre remboursement or CLR)